BLESSEDTIMONY

Be A Blessing And Share Your Testimony

RICO E. LANE

Copyright © 2018 by Rico E. Lane

All rights reserved. No part of this publication may be reproduced, distributed or transmitted in any form or by any means, without prior written permission from the author.

TABLE OF CONTENTS

CHAPTER 1

INTRODUCTION

If you were to type "Why is the Bible so" into a Google search, the top five results would yield confusing, important, badly written, hard to understand, and sometimes poorly written. This is a clear indication that most people are searching for an understanding of the Bible but struggle because it is so confusing. More importantly, they are searching for a relationship with the creator but find it difficult because not only does it require faith, but it also requires you to decipher a book that is written in a manner that is difficult for the average person to understand. In addition to a difficult to understand the Bible, the Pastor delivers a message in a prehistoric manner while the congregation sits and listens. However, in a brick and mortar school or university, the teacher or professor has a facilitated discussion with the students. This gives them the opportunity to interact with the teacher and answer any questions they may have. What good is it to get information that you do not understand and cannot ask questions about without being viewed as unruly or being judged for your misunderstanding?

Now, of course, you could save your question for Bible study, ask a friend, or try and reach the Pastor at a later date (if he or she is available), but what if they are discussing a different topic at Bible study? Or what if your friend provided you with the wrong information? What if the Pastor is busy or you forget your questions by the time someone is available to discuss the matter with you? You could also ask God for understanding, but if you are anything like I was, (I could not understand when God was actually speaking to me), it won't help answer your questions. This puts you back at square one where you need to turn to your Bible which we already identified is challenging to understand.

Throughout my journey to earn my master's degree in Adult Education, I found that it is vital to create a learning environment that motivates the learner to want to learn the information. For me, I am able to get a better understanding when I can ask questions, interact with the instructor and peers, and when examples are provided. This paint a picture in my head which results in me getting a better understanding of the intended information. This is the foundation of Blessedtimony.

Just as it sounds, Blessedtimony is about Blessings and Testimonies. The objective is to help people better understand the Holy Bible and God's grace by providing real- world examples (or their personal Blessings/Testimonies). For example, the King James Version (KJV) of Luke 12:48 states: *"But he that knew not, and did commit things worthy of stripes, shall be beaten with few stripes. For unto whomsoever much is given, of him shall be much required; and to whom men have committed much, of him they will ask the more."* For someone like me, this passage can be confusing and misunderstanding. However, if someone who already understands this scripture (a mature Christian or a Pastor for example) provided a personal experience (or real-world example), it could help the reader better understand the meaning of the scripture. Here is my understanding and Blessedtimony for Luke 12:48:

The more you earn, receive, or know; the more responsibility you will have or the more you will have to deal with. This has manifested in my life through my military experience. The more rank you earn, the more responsibility you have. The more that is placed in your hand, the more you have to deal with and manage. The military pays you more as you move up in rank because you have demonstrated that you can handle more responsibilities and are able to face pressures, problems, a n d responsibilities that will arise in the future. I went from being an Enlisted member in the United States Air Force (USAF) with only a High School Diploma, to a Commissioned Officer with a master's degree in Adult Education and responsible for the training of America's future UASF Commissioned Officers. I earned more money but obtained more responsibility. In addition to gaining more responsibility and being asked to do more, if I fail to do what I know I am supposed to do, my punishment, discipline, or even consequences will be greater than someone who I outrank (or someone who does not know better). Therefore, Jesus is saying that we all are responsible for knowing and living by his word and will be held accountable if we do not, but the person that knows more or responsible for more (let's say a Pastor as an example) is held to a higher standard.

I honestly believe that God has called me to create Blessedtimony to help people across the world build a relationship with him built on love, a true understanding of grace, and not one based on a fear of going to hell. My mission is to provide a safe and judgment-free social community for all people to gain a better understanding of the Holy Bible. The book you are about to embark on is the first step towards achieving this mission. My vision is for Blessedtimony to become a global community where people at different stages in their relationship with God can come together for support, fellowship, and answers to questions that they have about their faith.

Far too many people have pushed away from God because they feel they are not welcomed in the church or fear they will be judged if they are not perfect. It is crucial for them to realize that we cannot change our sinful ways without Jesus; and if Christians push them away, how will they build a relationship with Jesus? It is not our job to judge people (or drive them away) for their sin because *we all sin and we all fall short of the glory of God* (Romans 3:23). However, it is our responsibility to share the gospel of Christ so that we all have the opportunity to repent for (or turn away from) our sins and live a life that honors God (John 4:1-26). Therefore, Blessedtimony is for anyone who is willing to listen or interact respectfully, regardless of their current beliefs or relationship with God because he has the ability to change their beliefs and hearts (Ezekiel 36:26-27).

Before we move forward in the book, it is essential that I provide an explanation of what to expect because it is most likely written differently than any other book you may have read. Each chapter of the book will begin with a KJV bible scripture, then my interpretation of that bible scripture and finally, I will continue on with my Blessedtimony and tell my story that relates to that scripture. It is safe to consider this as a non-fiction educational biography because I will use my story to help educate you on how to identify Jesus Christ in your life.

It is important to mention that although I have a master's degree in Adult Education, I am not a Pastor or an expert on the bible. In fact, Blessedtimony was created because I struggled with believing in God and asked my family members to provide real-world examples of how they knew God was real. I was always taught that if you have a question, others might have that same question, so you should ask out loud. Blessedtimony is me asking out loud because I believe that if I struggled with this, others might feel the same. As I started coming up with ideas for a mobile application for Blessedtimony God started revealing himself to me, and he still is as I write this. 1 Thessalonians 5:9-11 tells us "For God hath not appointed us to wrath, but to obtain salvation by our Lord Jesus Christ, who died for us, that, whether we wake or sleep, we should live together with him. Wherefore comfort yourselves together, and edify one another, even as also ye do." Therefore, these are my personal opinions (backed by bible scriptures) on how I believe God is operating in my life. If my Blessedtimony can help just one person come to know Jesus, then I will consider that a success because before this I was surely on my way to hell for simply not believing.

Finally, "If any of you lack wisdom, let him ask of God, that giveth to all men liberally, and upbraideth not (without rebuke or blame); and it shall be given him" (James 1:5). With that being said, before we transition to my Blessedtimony I would like to invite you to say the following prayer, asking God for understanding so we can go into this reading with the intent to obtain the truth that God wants us to retain:

Heavenly Father, we come to You in the wonderful and powerful name of Jesus. Thank You for the opportunity for us to come together and share Your Word and the truths that it contains. We ask that You open our ears, hearts, and minds, so that we hear the truth, know the truth, and retain the truth. Please protect us from any preconceived bias we may have, and from our own internal voices so that they do not allow us to be death to the still small voice of Your Holy Spirit. Heavenly Father, we ask that we do not retain any error or anything that is not in line with Your truth. Please allow us to grow closer in our relationship with You and in Your grace. Finally, Father, as we read the following and couple it with Your written Word in the Holy Bible, we ask that you reveal Your will and calling on our lives. In Jesus name, we pray, Amen!

CHAPTER 2

PROVERBS 22:6

"Train up a child in the way he should go: and when he is old, he will not depart from it" (KJV)

Although this scripture seems straight forward, many mistakenly believe it is a direct promise from God that if you raise your child a certain way, they will maintain a relationship with God. When you get a better understanding of the context of "train," it is easier to see that this scripture is really saying teach your children to call upon God when in need and when they grow old, they will remember (or know how) to call upon him for their needs. Personally, I believe no matter how much someone who actually knows (or been taught) about the grace of God seems to "stray away", deep down there is something in them that makes them continue to call upon him for help even if they confess that they do not believe or struggle with their faith.

Allow me to take you on a journey in the past to when I was a young boy growing up in Atlanta GA. My Mom had me when she was only 16 years old. To say that my father was abusive to my mother would be an understatement, and I just mention him to say that he was not in my life not only due to death in prison but also due to the safety of my Mom and me. You will have to stay tuned in for my Mom's Blessedtimony for that story, but due to the circumstances I was born in, my God-fearing Grandmother took on the responsibility of ensuring I learned about Jesus.

I am so thankful she made me go to church all those Sundays when I just wanted to sleep in. I remember that she was very active in the church as a Sunday school teacher and it made me proud to tell all the other kids that it was my Grandma who was teaching us. She always made sure, I participated in church events, put me in Christian summer camps, and made sure that I knew that Jesus Christ died on the cross for my sins. I learned about Jesus at such an early age, so I really did not have an accurate idea of what sin really was. However, I quickly learned what it was when I found out the truth about my father because the day, I found out it changed me for the worse.

I can't remember the exact age but if I had to guess I would say up until about 8 or 9 years old I thought that my sister's dad was my dad as well. My Mom married him when I was so young that I did not know that he was not my real father. Well, when they decided to call it quits, he would still have my sister and me over for visits, but when I would visit, I could tell that he treated me differently from my sister. Maybe he didn't think his favoritism was blatant, but it was, I didn't understand why though. He was definitely stricter on me, and I always seemed to be the one who got in trouble when my sister and I would do the same things. Eventually, (right around the time my Mom met my brother's dad) the man I thought was my real father stopped allowing me to visit him. I could remember being so sad and wondering why he didn't want me, and he only wanted to see my sister. I don't know if it hurt my Mom too much to tell me the truth because I asked her why he treated me the way he did, and I must have blocked it out because I don't remember her response. I just know she didn't tell me the truth.

However, my Great Grandmother did not appreciate the way I was being treated at all. When my Mom and my brother's dad started getting serious, my mother was planning on moving to Virginia to live with him because he was stationed up there for the military. I was supposed to stay at my "dad's" house, but it was apparent that I was not wanted there (even though I did not know why at the time), so I finished out my school year at my Great Grandma's house before I moved to Virginia with my Mom. While living with my Great Grandma, she told me the truth about my father and that my sister's dad is not my real father.

Words cannot express the way I felt and honestly, I believe that sparked my true awareness of sin and was the beginning of my struggle with my relationship with men in my life and God. I can remember getting into fights after this, hating any man that came into my life because I was just counting down the days until they left as well, and I was very jealous of anyone who had a father in their life. I had to teach myself to play football, and I would get so angry when I saw other kids practicing with their fathers. This also made it very awkward for me to tell males that I love them because I never had a father-son relationship. Till this day I struggle to tell my Uncle, Brother, Sons, and Stepdad that I love them because it makes me uncomfortable even though I love them all. It is something that I'm still working on to this day.

Up until this point, there was no doubt to me that God was real and that he loved me, but I turned to an angry, jealous, and very competitive person (especially for my Mother's love). I questioned if God was even real and if he was if he cared for me. People would tell their testimonies on how God spoke to them and what he had done in their life, things I did not think I could relate to. I would try to talk to him and honestly felt like I did not get an answer or any sort of response. I did not understand the way God spoke to believers back then, and I did not know how to discern between the voice of God and the voice of the devil. I would ask my Grandma why God spoke to some people and not me, how I would know if it is not really the devil who is talking to me, why would God send his children to hell if he loves them, and so on. So, in my opinion, I started to believe God was just another father that was not around. However, this was apparently where the devil wanted me because God had a calling on my life that I could not see at that time, a calling that I just started to notice recently (even as I write this book). Because life is a process and I am not done growing yet.

I can't remember exactly when and how the conversation went, but my grandmother told me that God said to her that I would be a Pastor one day. She also stated that the devil would do everything in his power to stop me from reaching my true calling in life. It sounded a bit scary back then, the idea of having a predetermined path that led to me being a teacher because when it came to the scriptures, I was lost and I could not imagine a situation where I would have to help someone else understand the scriptures. Honestly, I could not believe her and sometimes felt like I did everything in my power to stay away from this calling as well. Discovering the truth about my father made me so angry, confused, and unsure of my identity (because I did not know him and what I had heard about him made me believe that I did not want to know him) that I turned to music, TV, rappers, actors, and women to help me identify with who I am. However, thanks to my Grandma introducing me to Jesus and other strong Christians in my life as a child, deep down I knew to always call on Jesus in my time of need. Even as I grew, and my faith weakened, something in me always called on Jesus when I was afraid, depressed, angry, and also grateful for the good in my life. Some people believe that raising children in line with a particular religion robs them of the chance to make their own choices, but I do not think that applied to me. I made my decisions, left the fellowship of believers, at one point I even doubted the existence of God, doubted his love for me. Some might also believe that children raised in the church don't have their own salvation stories; however, I do not think that is true. I was free to branch off, to drift away from the church and God but when I began building my relationship with God, it wasn't because I was conditioned to. It was because I knew what his impact on my life and the love that he has for me is because I knew what happened when I branched out.

As you can see, the scripture does not promise if you teach them (your children) they will automatically believe in Christ: however, it does plant that seed, and regardless what the child may say or believe about Christ, they will remember that they can turn to Jesus in their time of need. It tells you that no matter what, the children will always have the knowledge that God is a safe haven for them. I am so grateful I had this foundation because without it I am not sure how my life would have turned out. The fact that I had people praying over me and teaching me about Jesus allowed me to be covered by his grace even during my time of weak faith.

CHAPTER 3

2 CHRONICLES 15:2-4

"And he went out to meet Asa, and said unto him, Hear ye me, Asa, and all Judah and Benjamin; The Lord is with you, while ye be with him; and if ye seek him, he will be found of you; but if ye forsake him, he will forsake you" (KJV)

This particular scripture is not hard for me to comprehend but just raises questions that I struggle with. For example, does it contradict other scriptures that say the Lord will not forsake you (Psalm 94:14 or 1 Samuel 12:22), or if we are all sinners and we are told to come to God as we are then how will we have access to him if he has forsaken us? However, after a lot of prayer and research, I come to the following conclusion on this scripture. First, the good thing about God is that he gives us a choice on who/what we want to serve. Therefore, if we chose him as our God, he is with us, and if we seek him, he will make himself known to us. However, if we choose to serve another god (i.e., Satan, Money, our selves, or no god at all) then he is not with us (by our choice) resulting in him leaving us to our own devices and making it difficult if not impossible to hear from him in addition to having to deal with the consequences of sin. Therefore "forsake" in this sense does not mean that God will send troubles your way, it means that although God loves you, he will not force you to love him in return because that would negate the effects of love. Love is not a selfish emotion, at least God's love is not a selfish emotion, he has given us choices, and he knows that man will not always choose him. However, God cannot bear the sight of sin, he cannot bear to watch the people he loves so much sin over and over again, so he gives us space. He sends us signs, he tries to speak to us in hopes that we will leave sin and seek him, because he is always right there, waiting for us to seek him. It is all because of love.

The good news is that when Jesus died on the cross, he paid for our sins, and with the understanding of the law, we have knowledge of what sin is and a realization of the fact that no matter how hard we try we are still going to sin. Once we get to a point where we realize that we cannot get a handle on our sin without God, we will seek him wholeheartedly, and then he will reveal himself to us. Getting back to my story, at this point in my life I had grown into a teenager, and my sinful nature started to manifest even more in my life. Don't get me wrong, I wasn't terrible, but I also was not living a life pleasing to God. It was like I was two different people because, on the one hand, I was this God-fearing honor student who loved to play football. On the other, I hung out with a group of friends who did not have my best interest at heart and my lust for females overpowered my better judgment. These two sides of my personality seemed to be at war, always fighting for dominion, always trying to make me see that one way was better than the other. It was obvious that I could not keep living that double life, that I would have to choose, but how was I to know which the right choice would be.

I have always been a bit of a lady's man; my mother says I got it from my Grandpa. My Grandpa died when I was a young boy, but I remember looking up to him because he dressed nice (he was either in all Nike or all Louis Vuitton), and he had a lot of women especially for an older man. Therefore, being compared to him I felt like I had shoes to fill, and without a father, I would look to people I saw in the media for my guidance on how to live. I honestly felt like I was a mix between Martin Lawrence and DMX (Earl Simmons). See I learned at an early age if you make a woman feel protected and make her laugh you could make her fall in love with you. What better way to do that then to be funny like Martin Lawrence but also have a rough side like DMX. This worked in my favor until I experienced two heartbreaks back to back.

The first heartbreak was from my High school sweetheart, I won't mention her name, but I am sure if she ever reads this, she would know who I am speaking of. I actually loved this girl because not only was she gorgeous, she was smart and a Christian. When we met and started dating, we took things very slow, but I was just happy to be called her boyfriend, so I was good with that. As a teenage boy who was exposed to the media we had at that time, it wasn't easy to take it slow with anyone, but I did it for her. There was a certain kind of lifestyle that was promoted by the media, the one with fast cars, money, and sex. It was a bit hard for me to resist the lure that life offered, mainly because I was a teenager who was not even sure that he wanted to resist and that is before you factor in the peer pressure. I was also going to church and showing an interest in God because it was something I was used to, a routine of sorts, I was raised that way and so was my girlfriend. However, things changed when she went to Jamaica for the summer. We only spoke once the entire time she was out there, and I had a hard time dealing with this, absence can either kill a relationship or strengthen its bonds, and even teenaged me knew that the distance that had begun to stretch out between my girlfriend and I was not just physical. To make things worse, I met a female friend at the job I was working at the time.

Now this female friend was dating a top-rated football player who was on his way to playing college football and eventually the NFL. Needless to say, he got a lot of attention, not only from college scouts but girls as well. This made my friend sad, and we would talk to each other about our relationship problems. It was a dangerous situation that we had found ourselves in, two teens with relationship woes and nothing else but time to talk about them. This friend was also one of the very few positive friends I had, and when she introduced me to her other friends for the first time in my life, I felt like I had the kind of friends you see on the television show "Saved by the Bell." A good circle of friends, it was nice to have that, to feel a sense of belonging. We did things that I usually wouldn't do, and her parents were very educated and would talk to me about getting into college and having a better future for myself (something very few people in my life encouraged me to do). Due to this exciting new life, I got very close to this new friend and depended on her for support when I needed it. Looking back at the memories now, I can't help but wonder if I depended on her too much, if somehow that dependence had a hand in the events that followed.

Jumping to the end of the summer, my girlfriend returned, and I was so excited to see her, excited to hear about her trip and introduce her to my new circle of friends. However, that excitement quickly came to an end when she told me she wanted to break up and focus on her relationship with God. This crushed me, I could not believe I had dedicated so much time waiting on her just to get dumped unceremoniously when she returned. To make matters worse to deal with my pain I turned to my female friend for comfort (a reoccurring theme that continued to happen in my life by the way) instead of God. Honestly, the excuse my girlfriend used to dump me was God, so that definitely made me not want to turn to him, it made me resent him a little bit, I needed someone to blame and who better than him to shoulder the blame? Just as I was getting dumped by my girlfriend, my female friend broke up with her football superstar boyfriend, I did not understand their relationship back then, so I wanted to believe it was truly over even when all signs pointed to the opposite. So, we decided to go to the movies to get our mind off of our heartbreak and even though she told me she loved him and that she would always go back to him whenever he asked, that night we made the biggest mistake and went from friends to dating. Once again, I was all in, I didn't need my safety brakes, I mean she was the perfect girl, well at least I thought she was the perfect girl for me back then. I could tell her anything, she wanted nothing but positive things for me, her friends and family were great, they seemed to accept me; it was as if I was always part of her little circle and she knew everything about me.

Our relationship had not even lasted two weeks before she decided she wanted to be back with her ex-boyfriend and I could have sworn my world was about to end. It was not as if she had not warned me of that possibility, but maybe I believed that possibility would never become a reality because the breakup hit me hard. I begged God to help me, but for the life of me, I did not get an answer at all. The more I felt ignored from God the worse I got, I became heartless, and I really didn't care for women. All this happen around the time I got my first car and school was just starting back up. When I got to school as a varsity football player with a car, it seemed like that was all it took to make me popular, to make me that guy who turned heads when he drove in or walked down the school hallway. I was also the guy who used to date one of the prettiest girls in school, and at that time I also found out that a lot of girls had a crush on me. At this point God was one of the last things I thought about, I didn't think I needed him, I was at the top of my game, it felt like I was on top of the world and no one could bring me down. I was so full of myself and I "talked" to as many girls as I could handle, I was finally living part of the life that the media praised so much, but somehow it felt like a hollow kind of victory. I did not have any feelings for any of the girls I talked to because all I could think about is how the two girls, I loved broke my heart. Looking back now, I am afraid that I could have hurt those girls with my indifference; it was not fair to them that in my quest to hide my heartache, I might have inflicted some more on others.

Things really started to get interesting because the girl who dumped me all of a sudden wanted to get back together and at the same time, I was still friends with the other female friend who also broke my heart. I don't know why that happened, but it was like they didn't want me until the other one did, it was like a weird game of catch. I played into it, justifying my actions to my girlfriend by saying my friend was there for me when she wasn't and if we were going to be together, she had to accept that I was going to remain friends with her. To make matters worse I ended up taking my girlfriend's virginity and to be honest I don't think she was really ready for that step (primarily because of her relationship with God), but she did it so that she could keep me from doing it with other girls. It was not an ideal relationship, and to this day I feel sorry for how things turned out with her because not only did I stop seeking God, so did she. I felt like I was responsible for ruining her relationship with God, I am incredibly sorry about that, and I pray that she found her way back.

Eventually, I ended up losing my girlfriend for good because I was still going back and forth with my female friend and other girls. It was actually a good move on her part because I am not sure she was good for me, I am also not sure that I was good for her either. After multiple let downs from her and other girls, I got to a point where I really did not trust females at all. I brought those trust issues into almost all my interactions with women, and it did not help that I also saw my Mom go through different relationships, so I felt like maybe it was normal to love someone for a while and then lose them.

I ended up meeting a very close friend that I am still friends with to this day. Not to go into details but he and I did a lot of things we shouldn't have, but his father is a preacher.

So, we would attend his dad's church, and I could remember for the first time in a long time I sought God. I put my all into living a life that was pleasing to him and start feeling good about my relationship with God. I was attending church regularly, praying, and fellowshipping with other Christians and it felt good.

At times I felt like I would hear from God, but to be honest, I was not a hundred percent sure, but at least I was trying to do the right thing. I honestly believe that when I was going through my two heartbreaks, I chose not to follow God and he allowed it; therefore, he had "forsaken" me. I went through a lot of heartbreak and got into trouble from time to time due to the consequences of my sin, although I did not know that was the reason for my troubles at the time.

Then I started to seek him again, and he started revealing himself in my life again because I realized that I needed him in my life to help me make important decisions. The only issue is that I allowed my lust for women to take me away from God. When I would purposely do what I knew was a sin I would feel guilty and not want to go to church, almost like I had judged myself already and found myself unworthy to be in God's presence, a decision I shouldn't have made. Similar to how Adam and Eve felt after they ate from the tree of knowledge, hid from God, and we all know what that resulted in (see Genesis 3:23).

This resulted in me not seeking God, which resulted in me not being able to hear from him. By our choice, we distance ourselves from God, and when we do this, he allows us to make that choice (we should always remember that God lets us make our own choices, our own mistakes not out of spite but out of love) resulting in him distancing himself from us. However, I believe he does this because sin displeases him, and also it forces us to realize that we need him to get through the trials in our life. Once we realize we need him, he is right back there ready to forgive and love us.

CHAPTER 4

MALACHI 4:6

"And he shall turn the heart of the fathers to the children, and the heart of the children to their fathers, lest I come and smite the earth with a curse." (KJV)

Malachi 4:6 is the very last verse in the Old Testament and is one that I can relate to very well. In this verse, Malachi provided a great transition from the old to the New Testament while he was pointing out failures and hypocrisy in people who were claiming to love and follow God but were also indulging in various forms of sin. Something I can relate to all too well. Malachi was prophesying of a coming day when the Lord will judge the wicked and save those who believe in him. He concludes chapter 4 by letting them know that a prophet (Elijah) will be sent to them before this day so that they may know and hear the word of God. When Elijah preaches to them, he will prepare them for this day to come and turn the father's heart toward children and the children's heart toward fathers.

Why is this important? This turning of the hearts is an example that anyone (but especially parents) can understand and is a prophecy of Grace as well. Allow me to explain the last part of the verse ("lest I come and smite the earth with a curse"). It is saying that in order to have mercy from the curse or be saved from this coming day, the people must change their ways. The example used is a father's relationship with his children, and I think this is a great example to use because although I believe it is meant for both mothers and fathers, we know that since women give birth to children, they already have a special bond with them. Maybe it is because of that reason that mothers seem so attuned to their children's moods and needs. Not all fathers have this bond with their children, and not all children's hearts are toward their parents. For example, some fathers are so worried about working and providing for their kids, that they neglect them (I will admit I have been guilty of this) and some fathers simply do not know how to have a close relationship with their children because they never had one with their fathers. This leads to a vicious cycle where their own children have the same problem when they get older. Some children have parents that love them dearly and want nothing but the best for them, but they are disobedient, disrespectful, and ungrateful for their parents, maybe because of some kind of misunderstanding or the other.

Malachi was urging the people to change their ways and turn their hearts toward their children so they can be saved. Using this type of relationship as an example puts it in a way people can understand the importance of this change. However, it is also a prophecy of what Jesus will come and do for us which is the perfect transition into the New Testament. There are many prophecies in the Old Testament pertaining to Jesus. He himself said that he had not come to nullify the Old Testament but to fulfill the words in it (Luke 24: 44). And to do that Jesus had to be nailed to the cross for our sins. Our sins turned us away from God, and God sent his only begotten Son to pay for those sins. Jesus turned his heart toward you through his Grace and as his children; you are to turn your heart to him as well.

This scripture hits home for me because I became a father at a very young age (19 years old) and it was the scariest but happiest day of my life when I welcomed my oldest Daughter into this world. I was so happy to be a dad, and I was determined to be a better one than my father. However, I was still a kid myself and not only did I not know how to be a father, I didn't know how to be a husband, and this showed in the events that followed. Allow me to catch you up to this point in my life.

As I discussed earlier, I have a weakness for women and was hurt pretty badly in High School by my first two loves. I moved on and started messing with a few other girls and to make a long story short, I broke up with a pretty serious girlfriend and used my first Wife as a rebound from this breakup. Now my first Wife had a way of getting what she wanted out of me, and things moved fast, and I mean really fast. I honestly can't remember how long we were dating before she got pregnant, but it could not have been a year. I mean I was barely out of high school, and we were expecting our first child. With me not having a dad, I was determined to be a good father to my child. I did not have a higher education, a good job, or a plan for my future, so I joined the United States Air Force (USAF) at the suggestion of my first Wife so I could make a living for my family.

I didn't want to join the military and get shipped across the world and not be able to take my family with me, so I asked for her hand in marriage. I figured what harm could it be, she is having my baby, and I want to be in my child's life, so we should go ahead and get married. I loved my first Wife but to be honest, I didn't love her the way the Bible said you should love your Wife. At this point in my life, I just loved women, and I loved the thought of being in love, that kind of love came without the trust or respect needed to build a solid foundation for a marriage. I was also scared to fully trust a woman because they always seemed to come and go, so if I am being honest, I was not fully invested into the marriage like I should have been. It would be unfair for me to blame anyone else but me for the way our marriage seemed to implode. One thing I knew for sure was that no one could tell me I did not love my baby girl. She meant the world to me, and my heart was definitely turned towards her.

However, even things that start with the best intentions can fall apart and was evidenced by my first marriage, even though we had a child to think about, things went really bad for her Mom and me. We would argue, fight, make threats, and were not a good example for my Daughter. Things got so bad that I had to make a decision not allow my Daughter to see us fight like that because I did not want her to think it was acceptable behavior in a relationship of any kind. However, this decision inadvertently turned my heart away from her and hers away from mine which is something I still regret to this day. You see, right as we were making the decision that we might not be meant to be together, she got pregnant with my first Son. I was happy we were going to have another child, but of course, that meant I had to step it up, there was more responsibility for us to shoulder.

In addition to ensuring I could provide for two kids, I had to deal with threats of not being able to see my kids as a revenge tactic for our failing marriage. It seemed like divorce was inevitable, but I did not want to lose my kids too. This stress took the focus off of my kids and onto my military career. I had to make sure I was a "good" Airman, and I progressed in my career so I could take care of the kids I had. I spent so much time making sure they were taken cared of financially that I lacked in being the father they needed me to be. How ironic was it that working to become a better provider created a rift between us? Maybe to them, it seemed like I didn't want to be around. This had caused a barrier between my Daughter and I that is still there to this day. From this, I would like to take this opportunity to say the following to all of my kids, but especially my first born:

- First off, daddy loves you, and nothing will ever change that.
- I will always be there for you even if I am not right there with you, so if you need me do not hesitate to ask.

- Although this is not an excuse, I did not have a dad to teach me how to be a dad, and I am doing the best I can, but I need you to be honest about my shortcomings as a father, and we can work on them together.

- I realized that I allowed my work, women, and other responsibilities to turn my heart away from you and I am going to spend the rest of my life trying to change that.

- I ask that you please forgive me and not turn your hearts away from me.

Needless to say, that marriage did not last; however, after many years of fighting, we did mature and learned to get along for the sake of our kids. It took us a while to get to the point that we are at now, but the good thing is I have the opportunity to be in my kids' lives. As I continue building my relationship with God, I will also work towards strengthening my relationship with my kids. Being a father that would please God will also help me be a child whose heart is turned towards him.

CHAPTER 5

JOHN 14:6

"Jesus saith unto him, I am the way, the truth, and the life: no man cometh unto the Father, but by me." (KJV)

John 14:6 is a part of scripture that has troubled me for a very long time. In this chapter, Jesus is informing his disciples that he is going to prepare a place for them in his father's house or in heaven with God (John 14:1-4). In this conversation, Jesus is also telling them in John 14:6 that he is the only way to the Father (God) and no man can get to the father but through Jesus. The reason why Jesus is the only way to the father is that the price for sin is death, and the price had been paid by someone blameless (Jesus). You see, when Jesus died for our sins, he was pure, but he took on our sins, thereby giving us a blank slate (Hebrews 9: 28).

In these times the only way to be in the presence of God was in a tabernacle and with an absence of imperfections, sacrificial blood (death) offering of bulls typically for the priest and flock (sheep, rams, birds) for the people. This sacrifice was how guilt, debt, sin was paid for before Jesus made the final sacrifice and died for our sins on the cross. Jesus was the last blood sacrifice so that when we die, our sin debt is covered, and we can join the Father in Heaven.

I honestly believe my issues with this particular scripture began to come to a head on my first deployment to Iraq. In the middle of my first Wife and I's marital issues, I got notified that I was going to deploy to Iraq as a Security Forces (SF) member. For those of you who are not familiar with SF, it is a police officer for the Air Force that has two main roles of security and law enforcement. In addition to going to Iraq, I was placed under an Army unit which surprised me because I was in the Air Force. A quick funny story, I used to make fun of my God-brother because he joined the Army and I would tease him about how he was going to be fighting in the war while I was back home getting all the women. Well not only did I deploy before he did, but I have also deployed more times than him as well. I even earned a medal from the military branch he enlisted in.

I could remember being afraid of what was to come on that deployment because the media has a way of making you think that everyone over there is a terrorist and is out to kill every American moving. To make matters worse, my Ex was pregnant with my Son, so I felt like it was God's way of making sure my name would carry on after I died in military battle. I really went in thinking I was going to die; I had said my goodbyes in my mind. Well needless to say I did not die on that trip to Iraq although I had some close calls. Instead, my perspective on life changed. Words cannot express what it was like in Iraq, it is one of those things where you have to be there to truly know, but the one thing I did take away was being grateful to be an American. It is easy to complain about the way our country is run and the "little" we have saved up in the bank, but there are actually people who have fewer things than we do and no hope of getting more.

In Southern Iraq, I witnessed kids and families so poor they lived in clay-like huts and took baths in ponds on the side of the road (the ponds seemed more like potholes filled with muddy water). Southern Iraq looked a lot like something you would see in a Christian or Bible movie. It was beautiful in a way when I stopped being afraid of getting ambushed and actually stopped to appreciate the beauty of my surroundings. In fact, I had the privilege of visiting the ancient

Ziggurat that was built by pagan worshipers to be closer to the moon which they believed was God and a place close to it was said to be the birthplace of the Biblical Father Abraham. I have not personally done research to confirm that it was, in fact, the actual birthplace of Abraham, but this is what was advertised. So, you can see why I said it looks like something right out of the Bible. You would think that being so close to places discussed in the Bible would make me get closer to God and thinking that walking through some of the places I had read about in the Bible would make me a stronger believer, but the opposite actually happened when I was out there.

I was actually cultured shocked because not everybody was a terrorist and not everyone meant to cause harm. In fact, I saw some of the most caring fathers in my life, which was something I was not used to, stable families and some people seemed kind. Some even seemed like they were pacifists, harmless, not because they could not cause harm, but because they did not want to harm anyone. When I would be on my security post, I witnessed fathers having picnics with their children, playing soccer, praying with them and teaching them. I observed them doing all types of things that a family should do. Yes, there were also bad people there that wanted to cause harm, but one thing that really stuck out to me was the way their religion (or relationship with Allah) was a significant part of their lives. You could not go anywhere that did not have a mosque or a place for them to stop and pray. It did not matter what they were doing, when it was prayer time you would hear it over these loudspeakers that played throughout the city, and they would stop and pray. Religion really was such a big part of their lives there; it seemed like one of the things that truly bound them together as a people (ironically also separated them).

As I witnessed this and reflected back on my Christianity, I asked God how he could send these people to hell. They do not believe Jesus died on the cross for our sins, but they loved him. Yes, they call him Allah and I call him God, but they are going to hell simply because they believe Jesus was a prophet but not the savior. I just could not wrap my head around this, and I got frustrated because I did not have the answers. I wanted God to talk to me so bad, and I felt like I was getting nowhere. I came to the conclusion (and I don't know where I got this from) that if there was a God, he was going to have to show me what the truth is because all I could see was many different religions all seeking salvation from a Father who refused to tell us the actual way to him. I really thought that it was incredibly unfair for any of the kind people who truly believed in any religion to go to hell just because they did not believe that Jesus is the Son of God.

Thankfully, I had people praying for me like my Mother and Grandmother, and God did not allow me to die in Iraq while feeling that way because I did not believe at that point. In fact, when I returned home, I stopped going to church, I stopped seeking God, and I just started trying to be the best person I could be but on my own accord. The funny thing about this is something in me still believed for the following reasons:

1. I was afraid to commit blasphemy and not be forgiven so I would say "I believed in God," but I just need him to show me. Perhaps in a way that was a form of hypocrisy; doing something just out of the fear of punishment, whatever the "punishment" was. In a way, a lot of Christians do this. Some people stay in the church only out of the fear of going to hell; some people even try to scare others into believing that way.

2. I would choose to pray to God only when I needed him due to being in some type of trouble or dealing with the consequences of my sin. It is something other Christians are also guilty of; only speaking to God when they needed something from him and in other

situations, they would believe that they know best. My actions did not show that I believed in God and although I did not know this at this point in my life, going back to 2 Chronicles I could not hear from God because I was not seeking him.

Later in life I realized that the reason Christianity (or believing Jesus died on the cross for our sins) is the only way to heaven because no matter what we do, no matter how much we pray, and no matter how many good works we commit, we cannot be in the presence of God as sinners. If you believe anything about God at all, you know that he hates sin. This is the very thing that got Satan kicked out of Heaven, and Adam and Eve put out of the Garden of Eden. Sin is something he cannot bear to look at, Isaiah 59:2 states:

"But your iniquities have separated between you and your God, and your sins have hid his face from you, that he will not hear."

Although I am not educated at all on other religions and could be wrong with this statement, without a way to pay for sin (and the Bible teaches us the only way is through death, not works) then how can they be in the presence of the Father? Again, we are not perfect people so at some point in our life we will sin, and if we do sin, the payment for that sin is death. Simply put, if we die without somehow paying the debt of that sin, we cannot be in the company of God. Thankfully, we have a sinless (absence of imperfection) sacrifice through Jesus to cover our debt. Acts 26:18 KJV states: *To open their eyes, and to turn them from darkness to light, and from the power of Satan unto God, that they may receive forgiveness of sins, and inheritance among them which are sanctified by faith that is in me.*

All you have to do is accept the free gift. Why do you have to accept it to be covered? Just like with any gift, if someone is giving you something, they can't give it to you against your will, you must be willing to accept it. Same with Jesus, it is not enough to merely acknowledge the gift. There is a place of conscious acceptance of the gift when it comes to activating the grace provided.

CHAPTER 6

DEUTERONOMY 8:17-18

"17: And thou say in thine heart, My power and the might of mine hand hath gotten me this wealth. 18: But thou shalt remember the Lord thy God: for it is he that giveth thee power to get wealth, that he may establish his covenant which he swore unto thy fathers, as it is this day" (KJV)

In Deuteronomy 8, Moses is reminding the Israelites of how even though God tested them in the desert for 40 years, he always took care of them and provided what they needed. Moses also warns them that once they enter the promised land and start receiving all the things God has promised their ancestors not to forget who made it all possible (God). This passage is telling us not to be deceived and think that all the talents, gifts, promotions, houses, cars, and any other blessings in our lives are there by our own doing. It is God that gives you the power, knowledge, skills, or whatever it is that you have that allowed you to get where you are in life. Everything that has been provided by God, it is for the believer to access the skills and claim the blessings available. If you read ahead in the chapter, you will see that Moses warns them that God is destroying other nations for the Israelites, but if they stop serving God and forget what he has done for them, they will be destroyed as well (or the things he is giving them will be taken away from them).

Catching you up to this point in my life, a number of things happened to me that is a minimal example of what is going on here in Deuteronomy 8:17-18. The first is while deployed to Iraq; I met my third Son's mother. She was a real Godsend, kind and easy to rely on. Now she came into my life at a time where I really needed her, and I was going through my mini version of being tested in the desert like the Israelites. The funny thing about that comparison is that I met her in the desert (Iraq). Anyhow, getting back to the story, I am grateful for her because she was always there for me and helped me get through a tough time in my life. A time that I was dealing with being in a foreign land, a time where I was being separated from my kids, my family and it was also a time where I was struggling financially. So, I would like to thank her for what she did for me, but she also met me at a time where I did not know how to be the man God called me to be, and I apologize for that. I was not the man she deserved for a while, and she was the kind of person who actually deserved the best that life had to offer because of the way she handled anything life had to throw at her. Just like I did with my female friend in High school, I'm afraid that I depended on her too much and that could have contributed to the end of our relationship. Our relationship ended shortly after my Son was born and this is where my Wife now comes into the story.

When I met my current Wife, I found my dream girl! When I was a child and pictured myself with a woman, my Wife was the kind of woman I would see. She is smart, confident, a great mother, so beautiful, and she has long pretty hair. She looked like a supermodel to me, and I fell for her the very first time I saw her. However, I was still trying to figure out my previous relationship when that happened. This caused many issues with my ex and my current Wife that I still have to deal with to this day. Now although my Wife was what I believe is the perfect woman for me, God was in no way involved in the foundation of our marriage, and this caused so many problems for us for a while. Although I was determined to be a different person in our relationship, forgetting to let God into our marriage was a mistake. I went into my marriage with her saying that I was going to stop this ugly cycle I have with women where after a few short years I don't want to be with them anymore, and I am proud to say that as I write this book my

Wife and I have been together for over nine years. Over nine wonderful years together, we have had our ups and downs, but we emerged as a stronger couple from it. This is the longest I have ever been with anybody, but I tell you there were a lot of times where I didn't think we were going to make it. If I am being honest, without God we would not have made it, and this is why me involving him in all parts of my life is so important. This is why I believe that no part of a believer's life that should be hidden from God, even decisions will have more impact when they include God in the decision-making process.

Somehow not only did we manage to stay together, but things also started to come around for me. See, when I was with my third son's mother I depended on her heavily, and when we decided to call it quits, I had to figure out how to take care of myself and basically grow up. I had to draw myself a life plan, had to figure out my career path because I no longer had the luxury of being able to depend on someone else, it was a process that made me a stronger and better person. I started going to school and building my credit. I was progressing in my military career. Things were going well for me at this point in my life, but I was not being faithful to Jesus at all. I was not into going to church on a regular basis. I would go to church every now and then, you know Christmas, Easter, or when my Mom would drag me to church with her. I had gotten to a point where I did not need Jesus. I was so angry that I felt like he had forsaken me or was another father that was not around, abandonment issues sprung back up. I was also making a name for myself in the Air Force and could finally provide for my family like my father never did for me. Finally, I was given the opportunity to change my career path from being an SF Member to a Contracting Officer.

A Contracting Officer is a buyer for the government. Only a warranted Contracting Officer can obligate the government's allotted funds from Congress. Switching over to this career field did some interesting things in my life. At this point, I was what I would call a "dumb-jock-cop." All I did was lift weights, drink, play sports, and hang out with my family and friends. Those things on their own aren't bad, but it was the fact that I did not seek to expand my skillset that made me a bit unprepared for the changes that switching my career field brought. I did not have any administrative or technological skills at all. I can remember not really knowing how to use Excel, PowerPoint, Word, and barely could check my emails. I thought for sure I was going to fail in this career field, but I did the opposite. I got my warrant to go from being a contracting buyer (worker bee) to a Contracting Officer (ability to sign contracts) in record time. It seemed that there really wasn't a milestone I could not cross with ease. I excelled through my military ranks, earned a bachelor's degree and got picked up for Officer Training School (OTS) at the first board I submitted to. If you know anything about getting selected for OTS in the Air Force, you know that it is very competitive and not everyone gets picked up. This put me into an entirely different tax bracket, and I was living life like people I would see as a kid and on TV. I can remember seeing people driving nice cars, and I would wonder what they would do for a living to be able to afford it. Well, I was finally one of those people myself, and it felt great to be self-sufficient and able to provide for my family. It felt great to own things, to know that I could get my kids whatever they wanted without having to take out a loan. I felt like my life was on track once again, and there was nothing that could bring me down.

Things were going well for me professionally but my relationship with my Wife and kids were failing, and I didn't even realize it. It seemed like we were at the edge of a precipice and the next move I made would determine how my marriage would go. It hit me like a ton of bricks that in my rush to establish a solid career path, I had neglected my relationship with my loved ones. Not only did I not realize this, but I was also foolish enough to think that all of my success was all my doing, I really felt that I got my success because I was that skilled, although there must have been officers just as qualified as I was. I got to a point where I put my faith in my military career more than I did God, after all, I believed it was my skill that had gotten me so far in life. I had forgotten the place of God in my life and underestimated the doors that his grace and favor had helped open for me. Pride, as they say, comes before a fall.

Once I got picked up to be an Officer, I knew I was going to retire from the military because I had already been in for 9 1/2 years when I was selected, and I was guaranteed to at least make Captain and earn a check on the first and fifteenth of every month. Retiring as a Captain would mean more money than if I retired at any rank on the enlisted side and I had a guaranteed check. So, it was easy to just rest on my laurels; I had money, I had a family, and I felt safe and secure with my career. Let's just say God showed me that he provided all the great opportunities I had (including my family) and without him, it could all be gone. I learned my lesson when it seemed like everything (career wise) was on the verge of falling apart. Luckily for me, God was there to catch me when I slipped.

Since I am still currently serving, I won't go into the details, but I had a wakeup call that let me know that the military was not as stable as I thought it was. As an Officer, one mistake can be the end of your career, and I made a mistake that could have cost me that career. I honestly believe that this was God's way of showing me that I needed to put my faith in him and not in man or worldly things. Just as Moses warned the Israelites, God provided me a warning so that I would remember where my gifts and talents come from. It was a humbling experience and one that I believe God built me up to be able to handle before it happened. If I weren't somewhat prepared to tackle disaster, it would have swept me off my feet, my career path and have the potential to derail my life. Read ahead to see how God finally revealed himself to me and put me on a journey to seek and get to know him better as well as uncover the purpose he had for me and renew my faith.

CHAPTER 7

ROMANS 12:2

"And be not conformed to this world: but be ye transformed by the renewing of your mind, that ye may prove what is that good, and acceptable, and perfect, will of God". (KJV)

In the book of Romans, Paul wrote to Gentile believers in Rome (a city he hoped to visit) to not only introduce himself but also to explain the Gospel and what it meant to live a life of a believer of Jesus Christ. The earlier chapters of Romans discuss how all are sinners, God's wrath towards sinners, and thankfully God's gracious sacrifice of Jesus for payment for man's sin. Chapter 12 kicks off by detailing how all the truths mentioned in the earlier chapters should make a difference in the personal lives of believers of Christ (or Christians). Therefore, Chapter 12:2 is saying do not change yourselves to be like the ways or people of this world (non-believers), but instead allow God to change you by renewing or changing the way you think. If you are willing to change your mind or way of thinking, you will be able to understand how to please God and follow his will for your life. For we are a chosen generation, a royal priesthood and a holy nation, we were called forth to show the power of the love of God to the world (1 Peter 2:9).

I am excited to tell my Blessedtimony on this scripture because I have so many examples of how this has manifested or proven to be true in my life. Anyone who has joined the military can attest to the fact that from day one in their Basic Military Training that they aim to change your way of thinking to match the military's way of thinking. They have a way of taking a young teenage thug and turning them into a respectful, dependable, accountable, and trustworthy citizen. They are able to get you to put your life on the line for your country by first changing the way you think. I believe that Christians should always keep the fact that their spirits have been renewed by grace in mind, this renewal should have an effect on the way we think and the way we interact with others.

However, for me, I want to go another route with this particular Blessedtimony. I would like to show you how this is what got me back on the path toward a lifelong relationship with Jesus. The funny thing about it is I was not even trying to change my thinking toward Jesus, the Heavenly Father just knew exactly what it would take for me to get there and it was an answer to a lifelong prayer I always said. See growing up in the church as a child, the church was scary. I was afraid of God, the devil, going to hell and so on. There was the image of God that was being preached about back then, that of a vengeful God who got angry easily and should be feared. Stories of his wrath were told; it seemed like the God who was spoken of in the Old Testament was the type to turn his back on men if they made mistakes.

This kind of mentality was the type that helped foster guilt in believers, where they would feel too guilty to go to church or pray because they had sinned. It was terrible because it has the effect of pushing believers away from their relationship with God one step at a time. One particular thing that scared me the most was when my Grandmother told me she has the ability to cast out Demons. In fact, that conversation alone with my Grandma is the reason why I never completely stopped believing there was a God although I questioned it at times. The stories she would tell me would scare me so bad that I begged God never to allow me to see a demon or to be in a situation where I would have to come face to face with true evil. Because that was what demons were to me; beings who were capable of true evil that enjoyed infecting human beings with their evil. In addition to this, my Grandmother, Mom, and other Christians would tell stories about how people had to be on their death bed, or hit "rock bottom," or lose everything before they could hear from God and get to know him. I did not want to be that way, I did not want to have a near-death experience or an experience with demons before I could do his will. Therefore, I would pray with every ounce of faith I had in me a prayer similar to the following:

"God, if you are real, please reveal yourself to me so I can be saved, go to heaven, and know for a fact that I am living my life the way you want me to. However, God, please don't make it to where I have to see demons, or come close to death, or lose people close to me for me to have to know you are real. In the name of Jesus, I pray Amen."

I want to confess to everyone who reads this, I honestly believe God answered that prayer, and I will tell you how. First off, anyone who knows me knows that I have always been a competitive athletic person. I take pride in being in good physical shape, but the older I got, the harder it was to keep my weight down. I lift weights all the time, and I was a muscular guy, but my waistline was always over 36 inches. In the Air Force, if your waist is smaller than 35 inches, you will get max points for that portion of your Physical Training (PT) Test. If it is over 35 inches, you start losing points which means that if you want a good PT score, you will have to run faster and do more push-ups and sit-ups. The push-ups and sit-ups were nothing to me, but that run was my next biggest weakness after my waist. I always tried my hardest to keep my waist small, so I didn't have to run as fast on my PT test. No matter what I did, I could not get my waistline smaller than 35 inches. I take that back, when I went to Officer Training School, I got down to a 33-inch waist, and that is only because we marched everywhere, we went, and we only had about 5 - 9 minutes to eat, and I am not a fast eater. Due to this, I basically starved myself the entire time I was in training. I could remember working out 2-3 times a day for 5 days a week and still not being able to drop my waistline. My problem was that I loved to eat, and I had to eat a lot to sustain my muscle gain. I felt like if I had to suffer through the hunger pains that I felt at Officer Training School, then I would never get back down to a waistline smaller than 35 inches. I realized that my PT score would suffer for that if I could not either run faster or get my waistline smaller.

I gave up on it and just settled for keeping my waist around 36 inches and worked on keeping my run time down as low as possible. Then one day, I came across this video on YouTube titled "Resiliency - Motivational Video," and it was a motivational speech by Dr. Eric Thomas on knowing your "why" and using it to keep going or fight back when life knocks you down. This video inspired me so much that when I talk to people who are ready to give up on something, I would refer to it, as an Air Force Reserve Officer Training Corps (AFROTC) instructor, I would use it to teach the cadets about resiliency. The crazy thing about it was that I didn't even connect it to me giving up on my weight loss goals. However, one day I needed motivation, I searched the video so that I could find out who the motivational speaker was. When I realized it was Eric Thomas, I start searching for more videos by him. In his videos, he would speak about not making excuses and making adjustments, how you need to change your mindset and that if you think you can't do something, then you won't be able to do it (just as Romans 12:2 talks about renewing your mind). In one of his videos, he discussed how some people would admit to only giving 70% or 80% and then wonder why they are not meeting their goals. In that video, Dr. Thomas hit my competitive chord and challenged the audience to give 120%, so that is precisely what I did. I said to myself, Eric Thomas talks a big game, I am going to put it to the test on something I said I could never do and if I succeed at that, I can succeed at anything. The following is what I did just in case you are struggling with your waistline like I was (please note this worked for me and I am not endorsing it or saying it will definitely work for you):

- I decided that I would give intermittent fasting a try. Intermittent fasting is where you fast during a set time of day and only eat in a specified window. My window was from 1:00 PM to 9:00 PM, the rest of the time I was fasting. If you are not familiar with intermittent fasting, there are plenty of YouTube videos that will explain it. However, this made it to where I was eating fewer calories a day because I had less time to eat. I would be so hungry by 1:00 PM that I would eat a huge meal and be full all the way until dinner time. Then I would eat another big meal before my window closed to hold me over until the next day. I would only drink water and plain black coffee during my fasting period.

- First thing every single morning I would listen to Eric Thomas, and from there I was introduced to other motivational speakers like Les Brown and Bill Alsbrook. I started my day off with positive motivational speeches that motivated me to push through with my fitness goals.

- I would work out 3-5 days a week in my fasting window. Yes, I would work out on an empty stomach; well a stomach full of only water and plain black coffee. The good thing about this is my body used my fat for energy, and when I needed more the coffee replaced any pre-workout I would typically use.

- Although intermittent fasting is advertised as a system where you don't have to change your diet to see results, I was on 120% mode, so I would only eat sweets on Saturdays for the first couple of months (that changed when the Girl Scouts Cookies became available), and I would meal prep my food for the week. This kept me away from fast food restaurants. I also cut sodas out for a long time (about 3-4 months), and I carried a water bottle around with me everywhere I went.

After doing this constantly, I started to notice a change, and it did not take long at all. At one point I was losing approximately five pounds a week. It was crazy because the more I lost, the more I changed my mind to believe that I can actually lose my gut. Another great thing about this was that I could still eat the food that I loved and didn't have to follow some crazy diet so I could keep this up for as long as I wanted. I started in November of 2017 by Jan 2018 I had lost 20 pounds. By May of 2018, I had gone from a starting weight of 232 down to 205 and a waistline measurement of 33 inches. I squeezed from 36 to 38 waist jeans to being comfortable in 34 waist jeans, and if it wasn't for my thighs, I could fit into a 32. This completely changed my mind, I realized that I could handle anything life decided to throw at me. I started setting career goals, personal goals, family goals, and I was reaching them. The confidence I gained in myself, never been so high.

At the same time, while doing all of this, I started to realize that Dr. Eric Thomas was a Pastor. His motivational speeches along with Les Brown and Billy Alsbrook were backed-up by the word of God. The sad thing about it is if I had realized that at first, I probably would not have listened because I had tried the Christian thing so many times and failed. I had listened to so many motivational speakers and read so many inspirational Christian texts, but it seemed like they did not get me anywhere, so I was a bit jaded on that subject. Maybe I would not have been able to reach the goals I had set for myself then just because I overlooked something that had the potential to be useful to me.

However, by the time I got to this point in my life, I had a different mindset. I felt like if what they had said worked for me, and if what they said was backed up by the word, then maybe I needed to take another look at my relationship with God. When I did this, with a new mindset, God started revealing things to me that I could not believe I couldn't see before. My relationship with God seemed to have gotten a fresh start, one that seemed better than how it was before, and I learned how to communicate better with God and listen for his guidance. Allow me to explain in further detail with the next Blessedtimony.

CHAPTER 8

JEREMIAH 29:11-13

"11 For I know the thoughts that I think toward you, saith the Lord, thoughts of peace, and not of evil, to give you an expected end." 12 Then shall ye call upon me, and ye shall go and pray unto me, and I will hearken unto you. 13 And ye shall seek me, and find me, when ye shall search for me with all your heart." (KJV)

This chapter in the book of Jeremiah highlights a letter from God (sent by Jeremiah) to the people who were taken from Jerusalem and held captive in Babylon by Nebuchadnezzar. In the letter, God instructs the people to settle in the land that they are being held captive in. By settle, God instructed them to build houses, grow food, marry and have children, and etc. God did not want his people to be diminished so that when the time came for him to set them free, they would not be easily subdued by their enemies. He promised them that their captivity was only temporary and that he would come back to set them free. He also warns them not to believe the message of the false prophets and not be fooled by the magic doers in Babylon, because they are not doing the Lord's will (but their own will). Finally, in verses 11-13, God reminds them that although they are being held captive, he is still in control, knows his plan for his people and his plan is one of peace, happiness, hope, and a good future. In a way, it was a reminder for them to continue to put their trust in him, that even in the strange land where it seemed like they would endure trials and tribulations, he would always be with them. Basically, it was a reminder that he is in control and has good plans for us even when things don't appear hopeful. When things seem bleak, and when it seems like there is no way out, we should remember that God is with us and he will always answer when we talk to him.

While studying this scripture, fear and doubt overcame me. I don't want to blame this on Satan because by nature our flesh desires sin (even Apostle Paul spoke of bringing his flesh under submission so that he would not fall short, 1 Corinthians 9: 27). Therefore, it could be my own guilt, but at the same time, it could have been Satan trying to get me to doubt my calling to do Blessedtimony. You see, I still have sin that I currently struggle with, and while reading this chapter, I start to wonder if I am actually called by God to bring Blessedtimony to his people. I mean, I am a sinner just as the prophets in Babylon, so am I not doing the will of God? But then, God reminded me of something; this Book is in the Old Testament and glory be to God that he has already sent someone to pay for my sins, Jesus Christ.

Galatians 2: 20 states: I am crucified with Christ: nevertheless, I live; yet not I, but Christ liveth in me: and the life which I now live in the flesh I live by the faith of the Son of God, who loved me and gave himself for me.

It basically means that this new life that believers have been given is the life of Christ, believing in him gives us access to the grace that has been provided. As long as I believe in Jesus, and repent (or ask for forgiveness and turn away) from my sins then I am forgiven, and I can rest assured that as long as I continue to seek him, he will reveal himself to me and his will for my life. God does not hold these things against his children and sins are truly forgiven once we ask for forgiveness for those sins. In all honesty, if it were not for Blessedtimony, I would not even be convinced of the fact that I sinned and maybe I would not know to seek forgiveness for my sins. I am thankful for the knowledge I have gotten from Blessedtimony and thankful for the people I have met through the platform and the things that I have learned from them. So, I will continue to learn about God, ask other Christians for guidance and prayer when I struggle and Blessedtimony is a vessel to do that.

I had to take a detour from the story to share that because I wanted all who read this to know how close I came to quit at this point. I really came close to not completing this book, but I am glad that I got over my fears and pressed on. I don't know who, but someone is going to get to know Jesus because of this and if I had stopped right here who knows how long that would have put them off from a relationship with Jesus. I am grateful for the opportunity to help anyone on their walk with God with my own Blessedtimonies.

Picking back up with Jeremiah 29:11-13 and my Blessedtimony for this scripture. Thinking about how my life has played out so far, I realized that God had a plan for me the entire time even though at times it didn't appear that way to me. I realized that everything in my life had been leading up to me becoming a teacher and starting Blessedtimony, even though I was unaware of that at the time.

Remember earlier in the book when I said God made sure I could handle the "wake up call" I experienced at work? I say this because it did not happen until after I started listening to motivational speakers like Eric Thomas, Les Brown and so on. I would have been unprepared for the wakeup call if I had not been building myself up spiritually for a while. My confidence level was up, I started listening to spiritual leaders as well and listening to God's word again, and I knew that I could do anything if I worked hard and not gave up because of my weight loss success as silly as that sounds. I guess that the fall hits a person harder when they are flying high, and the higher you are, the more devastated you feel when you fall down. So, when I went through what I did at work, I was depressed. I could not sleep, I was losing a lot more weight because I was not eating, and I was worried about how it would impact my career that I worked so hard at for over fourteen years. It really felt like I was in the dumps when it seemed like I was going to lose everything I had worked for. It seemed like I was on a downward spiral. Then one morning, I woke up and pulled up YouTube and started listening to motivational speakers and God revealed himself to me through the videos I was listening to. I began to see my relationship with God in a different light, I reflected more on the things I heard and made sure they had their scriptural backings right. It is important to make sure that the teachings that we imbibe and try to live our lives by, are backed by the scriptures, truly backed by the scriptures because there are some who warp the scriptures to suit their own purposes. As the Bible warns, we have to beware of false prophets (Matthew 7:15 states: Beware of false prophets, which come to you in sheep's clothing, but inwardly they are ravening wolves.) and pray for the gift of discerning of spirits (1 Corinthians 12: 10). Things started to become crystal clear the more that I learned, and God showed me that:

1. I was going to be able to move on from this minor bump in my career because that was all it was; a minor bump, something that would soon pass. It was not going to be the end of my world.

2. He allowed that to happen to me to show me that I had my faith in man and not in him; he did not send the bump to me though, and maybe if I had a solid relationship with him instead of trusting in man, I would have been able to avoid it.

3. He was the one who allowed me to have a very successful career because he had good, hopeful plans for my life and future, but if I don't follow him, I could lose it all. I had gotten a taste of what that could look like, and I did not want to go back to

living on the edge, and it felt right to trust in God, the process and the great plans he had for my life.

After I came to this realization, I began to have a deeper understanding, and other things started to be revealed to me. I began going through my memories and saw the things that had led me to where I was for what they were. I looked to the things that had made me the man I was, the things that helped form my personality. I thought back to how my Grandmother said I was going to be a Pastor one day and I just could not believe it. I remember how scared I was of the future that my Grandmother had envisioned for me, I remember how my misgivings about my parenting and my relationships with women shaped my life. Allow me to give you a recap on my life and how even though I could not see it, God has been allowing me to go down a path that could lead to me being a Pastor:

- As a kid, I really wanted to play in the NFL and due to my size and not enough commitment on my part that did not work out. I was a very good football player, but I blamed it on the fact that I did not have a dad. I thought that God didn't love me enough to allow me to join the NFL and any other excuse I could think of. In reality, I now see that if I did join the NFL, I would have more money that could help magnify the sins I already struggled with and it would have been even harder for me to seek or hear from God.

- He allowed me to join the United States Air Force instead. This provided a way for me to take care of my family, but also opened the doors to pay for my bachelor's and master's degree. While serving in the military, I still struggled with what I wanted to do with my life. My first plan was to play in the NFL and my second was to start my own business. Well when I went to school for my bachelors, I got a degree in Business Management because I was in Contracting and that degree fit with what I was doing. However, I struggled with the classes, and I did not enjoy my college experience at all. This also scared me away from following my second dream which was to own a business. I felt like I could barely pass my accounting class, and I would have to hire people and follow all these laws, so I basically talked myself out of starting a business.

- I took a few classes for my MBA and one day I realized that I am happiest when I am coaching little league sports, mentoring people, and teaching resiliency classes or training military troops. I dropped out of my MBA program, switched universities and pursued a master's degree in Adult Education. The classes were a lot more interesting, I wrote my papers with no issues, and I graduated with a 4.0. I realized that I wanted to teach adults for a living (similar to a Pastor like my Grandmother prophesied), and when I retire from the Air Force hopefully, I could land a teaching job for the government. This also motivated me to volunteer to be an instructor for Air Force ROTC. This was by far my favorite position I held in the Air Force.

- I started listening to motivational speakers and Pastors, started expanding my knowledge and that helped build my confidence back up and got me back into the word of God. At this point, I felt like if I put my mind to something and worked hard at it, I could do it. I felt like I had the backing of God in my endeavors since I started to involve him more in the decision-making process. Additionally, I started being more open to what the Bible had to say because some of its truths were manifesting in my life.

- I got a wakeup call at my job that forced me to rely on Jesus to help me through it and grow from it. In addition to realizing my faith was in the wrong place, I also realized that when I retire from the Air Force, I did not want to have "all my eggs in one basket" or put myself in a position where one person could take away my ability to support my family. I did not want to ever be in a situation where I would be back where I used to be, I did not want to ever be unable to provide for my children. See, at that point in my life, I knew that if I were to be put out of the military, my family would struggle. Although I would still like to teach when I retire, I decided during that situation that I would also be an entrepreneur and have my own business. Thanks to God for providing vessels and insight that could give me the confidence to pursue my dream of having my own business.

At that point in my life, I was hearing the word of God here and there but still not really seeking him. I was not consciously seeking him, maybe because I did not think I had to at the time. However, something happened that changed this. At first, I had an idea for an App called "Photoly-Awkward" that I wanted to create. The objective of this app is to get people to use their smartphones (the very thing that is supposed to connect us but is arguably making us more socially awkward) to encourage people to get out of the house and meet new people.

I came up with the idea while on vacation with my family, and I saw people taking selfies and pictures with each other. Meanwhile, I met a few people that I had similar things in common with and we left without connecting somehow. I had shared memories with those people, but I had no way of contacting them, no way to reconnect with the people smiling next to me in photos. Had this app been out, we could have captured our meeting with a picture and put a short description of who, what, and where we met. From that point, I could have simply stored the photo in a photo album in the App or used it to network with the people I met in the future. It just would have been nice to have a reminder of people I met while doing everyday activities.

I can remember one of my favorite memories at church with my Grandmother was when we would have to get up and greet/meet the other members. They would play this song, "Its Love, its love, its Love that makes the world go round, It's Love, God's Love, its love that makes the world go round." I had just envisioned my app doing this on a global scale for people. Allowing you to meet new people, reconnect with old acquaintances and document those shared experiences.

I bring this up to say that I was working on this app and not Blessedtimony, but one day my Grandfather sent out a group text message to about ten of our family members. I can't remember what scripture it was, but I just remember everyone thanking him for sending it and saying Amen, and I just did not agree with it or understood it at all. So, trying to be funny, I replied and asked if anyone could give the group an example of how this scripture had manifested in their life since they all seemed to agree and understand it so well. In all honesty, I didn't really want them to answer me. I just didn't believe they really understood or agreed with the scripture, but to my surprise, my Mom and my younger Brother had examples or Blessedtimonies of that scripture for their lives. A few days went by, and I was trying to figure out how I was going to make Photoly-Awkward happen and something within me spoke to me saying that I could make the interaction I had with my family into an app. So, at that point in time, I had two app ideas. Although out of the two ideas, I was more focused on the Photoly-Awkward app than the other. Again, not really taking it seriously I kept working on my other app, and God just kept bringing that interaction back to me.

Now in school, I learned that there are no stupid questions and you should ask your questions because someone else may have the same question as you. I started feeling this way about Blessedtimony, because if it helped me, then maybe other people are struggling with their faith and relationship with Jesus that could benefit from hearing how he worked in other people's lives. Hopefully, it will get them into reading the Word, seeing if they can find scriptures that manifested in their lives and the expressions of God's love that they had encountered (because this is what I started to do). I started reading and looking at commentaries, and then I felt like I had to do this app because God just kept putting it on my heart, and when I really began to listen, all the pieces started to come together. The thing that really tripped me out was that although I am not an ordained minister, and if in fact, I do deliver Blessedtimony, I would be doing what a Pastor does (teaching and tending to a flock like a Shepherd, the Blessedtimonies provided the teaching and Blessedtimony as a business being the flock). Now please don't think I am trying to call myself a Pastor or disrespect someone who went to school and earned the right to be called a Pastor. I am just saying it is another step (in addition to me realizing I love to teach and mentor people) in the direction of fulfilling what my Grandmother said God had revealed to her.

So, I started pursuing Blessedtimony, and my first meeting with an app developer was devastating. The developer quoted me an $80,000 estimate and then he said, "I would not pursue this because Christian Apps do not make that much money and do not get that much support and I believe God led you to me, so you wouldn't put yourself in a lot of debt you could not pay off". At first, he almost convinced me to give up because I just could not see how I could do it. But Jesus prepared me for this, he sent motivational speakers to remind me that, "life will knock you out, but you have to get back up" - Eric Thomas, that I am "Blessed and Unstoppable" - Billy Alsbrooks, and that I have to "make a deliberate, conscious effort to say yes to my dreams" - Les Brown. God also reminded me that I didn't need to worry if I could do it because if I could, I wouldn't need him and when it happens, he will get all the glory because I will know that it was him that made it happen. 2 Corinthians 12:9 (KJV) states "And he said unto me, My grace is sufficient for thee: for my strength is made perfect in weakness. Most gladly will I rather glory in my infirmities that the power of Christ may rest upon me." I rely on the grace of God to offset my weaknesses and help me through life. That night, I just prayed to God and said, "God I know you are calling me to do this, so if I am right, please create a path for me, and I will just keep on working towards it." It got easier when I got God involved, things started falling in place to where I was able to not only get Blessedtimony developed, but Photoly-Awkward as well and I can promise you all the glory goes to God because I could not have accomplished what I did in a short time frame (about 2 months) on my own.

Getting back to the Blessedtimony, with all that I have experienced in my life there were a lot of times when I felt like there was no way I was going to heaven. If God really existed, or if God did not love me enough to answer my prayers, but in reality, he placed me right where he wanted me so he could prepare me for his plan for my life (not mine). I am reminded of one of the songs we would sing in church; it was one of my favorite songs as a kid. "Jehovah-Jireh My Provider his grace is sufficient for me." I learned to stop worrying about what I wanted to do and just seek God because his grace is sufficient for me. No matter what, I went through in life, and no matter how much I struggled with my relationship with God, his grace has always made sure I had what I needed, and for the first time in my life, I can see that his plan for me is one of peace and not of evil. Although I still have a lot of room for improvement, I am at least willing to allowing God to help me turn away from my sin. However, this will be a life long journey.

CHAPTER 9

PHILIPPIANS 3:12-15

"12 Not as though I had already attained, either were already perfect: but I follow after, if that I may apprehend that for which also I am apprehended of Christ Jesus. 13 Brethren, I count not myself to have apprehended: but this one thing I do, forgetting those things which are behind, and reaching forth unto those things which are before, 14 I press toward the mark for the prize of the high calling of God in Christ Jesus. 15 Let us therefore, as many as be perfect, be thus minded: and if in anything ye be otherwise minded, God shall reveal even this unto you." (KJV)

This book in the Bible is a letter from Paul to the Philippians sending encouragement and a thank you for their support of him while he was imprisoned. In Chapter 3 of Philippians, Paul discussed how all of his success in life was nothing compared to the grace of Christ (being found righteous through his faith of Christ). Although Paul had an understanding of grace and was living the gospel, he admits that he still had a long way to go with his relationship with God. Verses 12-15 go into details on this by Paul saying he is not where God wants him to be, but he is continuously trying to get there because that is Jesus' will for him (and all of us). Then he admits in verse 13 that he has a long way to go, but he is not focusing on his past and in fact but doing the best he can to reach the goal of being what God wants for him. Finally, in verse 15 he encourages others who are mature in their faith to do the same, and he tells those who do not agree with him (or do not believe as he does) that God will make it clear to them."

God could not have revealed a better scripture for me to conclude my Blessedtimony with. I am not where God wants me to be in my relationship with him, and honestly, I am not even where I want to be. I still have things that I struggle with every day, and I debated whether I was worthy of being used by God to bring Blessedtimony to the world. Just like Paul, the one thing I do know is that I am doing my best to reach the goal of getting to heaven and being in the presence of God. There are things in my past that I am not proud of and I am sure there are going to be even more in my future. But Jesus has already paid for all of my sins (known and unknown), and because of that, I will do my best to live a life that is pleasing to him.

As Blessedtimony continues to grow, I ask that you do not put your faith in me to always do the right thing but in God that he will reveal his truth to you. I am still a babe in my relationship with him and have a lot to learn. All I know is God chose me to bring Blessedtimony to the world, and I am going to be obedient and do just that. If you know Paul's story, then you know he used to go by Saul. In those days it was common to have dual names but, in the Bible, he is referred by each name at two different walks in his relationship with Jesus. When he was Saul, he was murdering Christians, but he was saved, and he went from being Saul the sinner, to Paul a new person in Christ who spread the Gospel (See the Book of Acts Chapter 9 and 13). For me when I think of those "What would Jesus Do" bands I feel like Jesus was perfect, and it is hard for me to live up to him. However, I can identify with someone like Saul who is not perfect, but through Jesus Christ, he is made a new person and desire to live a life that is pleasing to God. Therefore, I try to live a life like Paul versus one like Saul, I try to bring my flesh under subjection as he did for a more efficient walk with God.

If you were to read the rest of the chapter (and I encourage you to do so), you would find that Paul concludes Chapter 3 with a call to action for the Philippians. He asks them to follow his example and strive to improve their relationship with God. He also encourages them to learn from others who are living the way he has taught them, but also knows that there are some who live like they are enemies of the cross and are proud of what they do. Paul wept as he describes them because their choices were leading to their destruction. I will admit that only a few months before I start writing this, I was one of those people. I sinned, I knew I sinned, and to be honest some of my sins I did not care that I did them and were, in fact, proud of it because it brought my flesh great pleasure. I am so grateful God started revealing himself to me before it was too late for me. I was headed on a path of destruction, but by the Grace of God I am saved, and all I had to do is believe. It is my prayer, hope, and goal that I can help anyone who wants to learn from my example so that they can also experience God's Grace. Therefore, I will conclude with a call to action just as Paul did in his letter to his friends.

CHAPTER 10

ACTS 2:42-47

"42 And they continued steadfastly in the apostles' doctrine and fellowship, and in breaking of bread, and in prayers. 43 And fear came upon every soul: and many wonders and signs were done by the apostles. 44 And all that believed were together, and had all things common; 45 sold their possessions and goods, and parted them to all men, as every man had need. 46 And they, continuing daily with one accord in the temple, and breaking bread from house to house, did eat their meat with gladness and singleness of heart, 47 Praising God, and having favour with all the people. And the Lord added to the church daily such as should be saved."

(KJV)

Acts of the Apostles is commonly referred to as just Acts, but it begins in chapter 1 with the resurrected Jesus giving a call to action to a small group of believers. Jesus commissioned them to spread his message of forgiveness and grace not only to Jerusalem but to the world (Acts 1:8). Chapter 2:42 - 47 gives a good summary of how they were successful at building their numbers but more importantly, helping people come to know Jesus Christ, their savior. Acts 2:42-47 explains how this community of believers fellowshipped together, ate together, prayed together, sold their possessions and goods so they could give to those in need. They took joy in each other's company, and every day they spent time together to worship and learn about God. They were respected by all the people because of how they praised God and because of this more and more people were being saved every day, and God added to their group.

This is the history of the Christian church and a lesson that I believe us as Christians need to be reminded of. I have personally met so many people who do not want to go to church because of how Christians have treated and judged them. However, in Acts Chapter 2 people were drawn to this community because let's face it, love, unity, and kindness are both attractive and contagious. When people are excited about something, others want a piece of the action.

The Bible says the Lord added to them daily and this is a blessing because that means more and more people were being saved. This is the objective of Blessedtimony and my call of action to you. Please do not mistake my intentions, I am not asking you to sell all of your belongings and give them away to those in need, nor am I trying to create a new church or religion. I am merely asking you to be a blessing, not to be judgmental to people who have not come to know Jesus yet, allow your kindness, generosity, and love to entice them to want to learn about Jesus and give their life to him. It is no coincidence that Jesus's new commandment before ascending to Heaven was for us to love one another just as he loved us (John 13:30).

Finally, be a blessing and share your testimony to provide an example of how even today God still works miracles in our lives, has a good plan for our future, and truly loves us more than we can ever imagine. Blessedtimony merely is a tool for us to be like the followers of Christ in Acts. Enabling us to create groups of people from across the world, and care for them, teach them, pray with them, share and be a blessing to them, take joy when they progress in life, and worship God together without limitations.

In today's society, it seems like Jesus is being taken out of every part of our lives. We can't talk about him at school, can't talk about him at work, we can't talk about him in public because you may offend someone. With Blessedtimony, we can talk about and praise him as much as we want. However, even if you don't want to become a member of the Blessedtimony community, I encourage you to be a part of a small group somewhere (in your church, with your family, a group of friends) because this is what will allow things to change in your life.

I will conclude by confirming this with the word of God. Colossians 3:15 (KJV) states: And let the peace of God rule in your hearts, to the which also ye are called in one body; and be ye thankful. This verse calls for unity in the church and asks Christians to keep the peace of God in their hearts. James 5:16-20 (KJV) states the following "16 Confess your faults one to another, and pray one for another, that ye may be healed. The effectual fervent prayer of a righteous man availeth much. 17 Elias was a man subject to like passions as we are, and he prayed earnestly that it might not rain: and it rained not on the earth by the space of three years and six months. 18 And he prayed again, and the heaven gave rain, and the earth brought forth her fruit. 19 Brethren, if any of you do err from the truth, and one convert him; 20 Let him know, that he which converteth the sinner from the error of his way shall save a soul from death and shall hide a multitude of sins". To put it in laymen terms, we are to:

- Tell each other of our wrongdoings, and then pray for each other. This will result in us being healed, and the Bible confirms that anyone that lives their life in a manner that pleases God can pray and miracles will happen (which is why Blessedtimony or any small group needs Christians that are strong in their faith).

- Then an example of the power of prayer was given by stating that Elias (or Elijah) was a man no different from us and his prayer stopped it from raining for three and a half years. Then he prayed that it would rain, and heaven provided rain, and their land grew crops.

- Finally, James 5 concludes by saying that if anyone strays away from the truth and someone helps that person back from their sins, they will have saved that person from eternal death and cause many sins to be forgiven.

Please do not judge and push people further away when they are struggling or straying away from the truth. That sort of behavior is a direct contrast to what Jesus did on earth, as evidenced by the company he kept; Jesus was not the type to judge. John 3: 17 states, "For God sent not his son into the world to condemn the world; but that the world through him might be saved." Instead, be an example of a way back to the truth. Be someone they are comfortable confessing their sins with because if they keep it to themselves, they miss the opportunity for prayer and as the Bible tells us, prayer is how we are healed. Therefore, I beg of you to be a blessing, share your testimony, and save someone, anyone from an eternity in hell. I ask this in Jesus name, Amen.

www.ingramcontent.com/pod-product-compliance
Lightning Source LLC
Chambersburg PA
CBHW061722250726
48657CB00002B/727